PAGAN PRAYERS

PAGAN PRAYERS

COLLECTED BY

MARAH ELLIS RYAN

•

AUTHOR OF

FOR THE SOUL OF RAFAEL, INDIAN LOVE LETTERS, ETC.

KALPAZ

ISBN: 978-93-5128-867-1(HB)

First Published in 1913
Indian Reprint in 2017

Published by

Kalpaz Publications
C-30, Satyawati Nagar,
Delhi – 110052
E-mail: kalpaz@hotmail.com
Website: kalpazpublications.com
Ph.: +91-9212142040

Cataloging in Publication Data—DK
Courtesy: D.K. Agencies (P) Ltd. <docinfo@dkagencies.com>

Pagan prayers / collected by Marah Ellis Ryan.
pages cm
Reprint. Originally published: Chicago : A. C. McClurg & Co., 1913.
ISBN 9789351288671

1. Prayers. I. Ryan, Marah Ellis, 1866-1934, compiler.

BL560.P34 2017 DDC 204.33 23

PREFACE

THIS little book of thoughts big, and thoughts childish, goes to the reader with the hope that it bears the little known fact that Ancient America had a written aboriginal literature—much of which was beautiful.

The Apache and the Navajo prayers are oral, transmitted from priest to priest through the centuries; but the Mexican are fragments, rescued from a wide literature by the learned and courageous Franciscan, Bernardino de Sahagun, in the Seventeenth century.

The first archbishop of Mexico took credit to himself for the burning, in one town, of 60,000 Mexican books and manuscripts on history, religion, law, medicine, astrology, genealogy and poetry. It was his part of the approved battle against the false gods. For four centuries he has had ardent imitators—which accounts for much.

The masked, dramatized prayers of the Indians of the Southwest of today, suggested to the compiler a key to ancient Mexican rituals where god or goddess replies directly to priest or suppliant. This is the one special liberty taken with the records—the deity or priest is placed as the Indian places him, in the temple of feast or sacrifice; while the Spanish records gave only the spoken words with little to indicate the ritual or the speakers.

The Peruvian had reached a higher spiritual and philosophic stage of culture before his annihilation, though at loss of the spontaneous poetic imagery, wistful or colorful, of the Mexican.

Such as they are, these prayers reflect the culture of both extinct and living primitive peoples of the world we call the New, and they go out for judgment side by side with the better known rituals of the world we call the Old.

M. E. R.

CONTENTS

PAGAN PRAYERS

ON THE WRITING OF A PRAYER OF PRAISE

(*Mexican*)

(This introduction to a volume of annals, written centuries ago by an unknown poet of ancient America, gives glimpse of the beauty of the native book craft, and the sacredness to them, of literature)

PAGAN PRAYERS

LIKE a red-winged heron of wonder, rising in flight, it shone.
The mist and the glow of the rainbow, it is there!
The harmony is as the tinkling turquoise bells on the silver drum: thus was a book of annals written and painted in colors.
I unwind my song!
I unwind my song like a string of jewels, all precious.

TO THE CREATIVE GOD

(*Accadian*)

(The Accadian was already a dead language in the Seventeenth Century, B. C.)

O LORD of Charms, Illustrious! who gives
Life to the Dead, the Merciful who lives,
And grants to hostile gods of Heaven return,
To homage render, worship thee, and learn
Obedience!
Thou who didst create mankind
In tenderness, thy love round us, oh wind!
The Merciful, the God with whom is Life
Establish us, O Lord, in darkest strife
O never may thy truth forgotten be.
May Accad's race forever worship thee!

APACHE PRAYER
(American)

STENATLIHAN, You are good!
I pray for a long life.
I pray for your good looks.
I pray for good breath.
I pray for good speech.
I pray for feet like yours to carry me through a long life.
I pray for a life like yours.
I walk with people, ahead of me all is well.
I pray for people to smile as long as I live.
I pray to live long.
I pray, I say, for a long life to live with you where the good people are.
I live in poverty.
I wish the people there to speak of goodness and to talk to me.
I wish you to divide your good things with me, as a brother.
Ahead of me is goodness, lead me on.

(Stenatlihan is the supreme sky goddess)

NAVAJO LITURGY

(*American*)

OH YOU!
Who dwell in the house made of the Dawn.
In the home of evening twilight.
In the house made of dark cloud,
In the house made of the he rains,
In the house made of the dark mist,
In the house made of the she rain,
In the house made of peace;
Where the dark mist curtains the door
The path to which is on the rainbow,
Where the zig-zag lightning on high it stands
Male deity divine!
With your moccasins of dark cloud, come to us!
With your headdress of dark cloud, come to us!
With clouds dark, your mind enveloping, come to us!

NAVAJO LITURGY
(*Continued*)

You above thunder dark, high-flying, come to us!
With cloud having shape at your feet, high-flying, come to us!
With the dark cloud over your head made of far darkness, high-flying, come to us!
With the far darkness made of the he rain over your head, high-flying, come to us!
With your head over mist-dark made of far darkness, high-flying, come to us!
With the she rain over your head, made of far darkness, high-flying, come to us!
With your head over zig-zag lightning far out-flung, high-flying, come to us!
With your head over far hanging rainbow, high-flying, come to us!

NAVAJO LITURGY
(Continued)

With clouds dark on the ends of
your wings, made of far darkness,
high-flying, come to us.
With the far darkness made of the
he rain on the ends of your wings,
high-flying, come to us!
With the dark mist on the ends of
your wings, made of far darkness,
high-flying, come to us!
With the far darkness made of the
she rain on the ends of your
wings, high-flying, come to us!
With zig-zag lightning flung out
afar on the ends of your wings,
high-flying, come to us!
With the rainbow hanging far on the
ends of your wings, high-flying,
come to us!
With the near darkness made of
dark cloud, of he rain, of dark
mist, of she rain, high-flying, come
to us!

NAVAJO LITURGY
(*Continued*)

In the earth darkness come to us!
With these also the foam to float
on the flowing water over the roots
of the great corn, that I wish.
Your sacrifice I have made,
For you the smoke have I prepared.
My feet for me restore,
My body for me restore,
My mind for me restore,
My voice for me restore,
This day your spell from me take
out,
This day your spell for me remove!
Away from me you have taken it!
Far off from me it is taken!
Far off you have done it.
In a way of beauty I recover,
Happily my eyes regain their power,
Happily for me the spell is taken off,
Imperious to pain I walk,

NAVAJO LITURGY
(*Continued*)

Feeling light within, I walk,
Thus happily you accomplish your tasks.
Happily the old men will regard you,
Happily the children will regard you,
Happily as they approach their homes they will regard you.
Happily may their trails home be in the way of peace.
Happily may all return!
With beauty before me I walk.
With beauty above me I walk.
With beauty it is finished!
With beauty again it is finished!

ADDRESS TO SUPREME DEITY

(*Assyrian*)

IN HEAVENS who is great? Thou alone art great!
On earth who is great? Thou alone art great!
When thy voice resounds in heaven, the gods fall prostrate!
When thy voice resounds on earth, the genii kiss the dust!

A PRAYER FOR THE DYING

(*Assyrian*)

BIND the sick man to Heaven, for from Earth he is being torn away!

Of the brave man who was so strong, his strength has departed.

Of the righteous servant, the force does not return,

In his bodily frame he lies dangerously ill.

But Ishtar, who in her dwelling, is grieved concerning him, descends from her mountain unvisited of men.

To the door of the sick man she comes.

The sick man listens!

Who is there? Who comes?

It is Ishtar, daughter of the Moon God!

A PRAYER FOR THE DYING
(Continued)

Like pure silver may his garment
 be shining white!
Like brass may he be radiant!
To the Sun, greatest of the gods,
 may he ascend!
And may the Sun, greatest of the
 gods, receive his soul into his
 holy hands!

BABYLONIAN PRAYER FOR HEALTH

(Exorcism of Spirits of Disease)

Tablet I

THE noxious god, the noxious spirit of the neck, the neck-spirit of the desert, the neck-spirit of the mountains, the neck-spirit of the sea, the neck-spirit of the morass, the noxious spirit of the city, this noxious wind which seizes the body and the health of the body.

Spirit of Heaven, remember! Spirit of Earth, remember!

Tablet V

He who makes an image which injures the man, an evil face, an evil eye, an evil mouth, an evil tongue, evil lips, an evil poison.

Spirit of Heaven, remember! Spirit of Earth, remember!

Tablet VI

The cruel spirit, the strong spirit of the head, the head-spirit that

BABYLONIAN PRAYER FOR HEALTH

(*Continued*)

departs not, the head-spirit that goes not forth, the head-spirit that will not go, the noxious head spirit.

Spirit of Heaven, remember! Spirit of Earth, remember!

Tablet VIII

May Nin-cigal, the wife of Nin-a'su, turn her face toward another place; may the noxious spirit go forth and seize another. May the propitious spirit and the propitious genii settle upon his body.

Spirit of Heaven, remember! Spirit of Earth, remember!

Tablet IX

May Nebs, the great steward, the recliner supreme among the gods, like the god who has begotten him, seize upon his head; against his life may he not break forth.

BABYLONIAN PRAYER FOR HEALTH
(*Continued*)

Spirit of Heaven, remember! Spirit of Earth, remember!

Tablet X

On the sick man by the sacrifice of mercy may perfect health shine like bronze; may the Sun-god give this man life; may Merodach, the eldest son of the deep, give him strength, prosperity and health.

Spirit of Heaven, remember! Spirit of Earth, remember!

PRAYER TO THE SUN

(*Chaldean*)

THE LORD has sent me;
the great god Hea, has sent me.

Thou, in thy course thou directest the human race

Cast upon him a ray of peace, and let it cure his suffering.

The man, son of his god, has laid before him his shortcomings and transgressions; his feet and hands are in pain, grievously defiled by disease.

Sun, to the lifting up of my hands pay attention; eat his food, receive the victim, give his god, for a support, to his hand!

By his order let his shortcomings be pardoned! Let his transgressions be blotted out!

May his troubles leave him! May he recover from his disease!

Give back life to the King!

PRAYER TO THE SUN

(Continued)

Then, on the day that he revives,
may thy sublimity envelop him!
Direct the King who is in subjection
to thee!
And me, the magician, thy humble
servant, direct me!

MAGICAL INCANTATION

(*Chaldean*)

I HAVE invoked thee, O Sun, in the midst of the high heavens.

Thou art in the shadow of the cedar, and thy feet rest on the summits.

The countries have called thee eagerly, they have directed their looks towards thee,

O Friend, thy brilliant light illuminates every land, overthrowing all that impedes thee, assemble the countries, for thou, O Sun, knowest their boundaries.

Thou who annihilatest falsehood, who dissipated the evil influence of wonders, omens, sorceries, dreams, evil apparitions, who turnest to a happy issue malicious designs, who annihilatest men and countries that devote themselves to fatal sorceries, I have taken refuge in thy presence.

MAGICAL INCANTATION
(*Continued*)

Do not allow those who make spells,
and are hardened, to arise.
Frighten their heart,
Settle also, O Sun, light of the great
gods
Right into my marrow, O Lords of
breath, that I may rejoice, even I.
May the gods who created me take
my hands!
Direct the breath of my mouth!
My hands direct them also, Lord,
light of the legions of the heavens.
Sun, O Judge!

CHINESE LITURGY

ONE in spirit,
We invoke thee!
Hail, Amit-abha of the world!
O would that our merciful teacher, Sakya-muni,
And our great Father Amit-abha
Would now descend and be present with us.
Would that the perfect compassionate heart would now draw near
And receive our offerings.
May the omnipotent and omniscient Holy Spirit
Come to us while we recite these divine sentences.

CHINESE PRAYER

I THE EMPEROR, have respectfully prepared this paper to inform the spirit of the sun, the spirit of the moon, the spirits of the five planets, of the stars, of the clouds, of the four seas, of the great rivers, of the present year,

That on the first of next month we shall reverently lead our officers and people to honor the great name of Shang-Ti.

We inform you beforehand, O ye celestial and terrestrial spirits, and will trouble you on our behalf, to exert your spiritual power, and display your vigorous efficacy, communicating our poor desire to Shang-Ti, praying him to accept our worship, and be pleased with the new title which we shall reverently present to him.

CHINESE PRAYER

(Continued)

Thou, O Ti, didst open the way for the forces of matter to operate;

Thou, O Spirit, didst produce the beautiful light of the sun and moon, that all thy creatures might be happy.

Thou hast vouchsafed to hear us, O Ti, for thou regardest us as thy children.

I, thy child, dull and ignorant, can poorly express my feelings.

Honorable is thy great name!

PRAYER OF TRANSFORMATION INTO A LOTUS
(*Egyptian*)

HAIL, thou lotus! Thou type of the god Nefer-Temu!

I am the man that knoweth you, and I know your names among those of the gods, the lords of the underworld, and I am one of you.

Grant ye that I may see the gods who are the divine guides in the underworld, and grant ye unto me a place in the underworld near unto the lords of Amentet.

Let me arrive at a habitation in the land of Tchesert, and receive me, O all ye gods, in the presence of the lords of eternity!

Grant that my soul may come forth whithersoever it pleaseth, and let it not be driven away from the presence of the great company of the gods!

A PRAYER FOR PRESERVATION OF THE HEART

(*Egyptian*)

MY HEART, my mother; my heart, my mother!

My heart of my existence upon earth!

May naught stand up to oppose me in judgment; may there be no opposition to me in the presence of the sovereign princes; may no evil be wrought against me in the presence of the gods; may there be no parting of thee from me in the presence of the great god, the lord of Amentet.

Homage to thee, O thou heart of Osiris—khent—Amentet! Homage to you, O my reins! Homage to you, O ye gods who dwell in the divine clouds, and who are exalted [or holy] by reason of your sceptres!

Speak ye fair words for the Osiris Auf-ankh, and make ye him to prosper before Nehebka. And be-

A PRAYER FOR PRESERVATION OF THE HEART
(*Continued*)

hold, though I be joined to the earth, and am in the mighty innermost part of heaven, let me remain on the earth and not die in Amentet, and let me remain a *khu* therein for ever and ever!

This prayer shall be recited over a basalt scarab, which shall be set in a gold setting, and it shall be placed inside the heart of the man (i. e., the dead) for whom the ceremonies of "opening the mouth" and of anointing with unguent have been performed.

And there shall be recited by way of magical charm the words:

"My heart, my mother! my heart, my mother! My heart of transformations!"

(Khu, a god of light)

HYMN TO AMUN-RA
(*Egyptian*)

HAIL to thee, Amun-Ra, Lord of the thrones of the earth, the oldest existence, ancient of heaven, support of all things;

Chief of the gods, lord of truth; father of the gods, maker of men and beasts and herbs; maker of all things above and below;

Deliverer of the sufferer and oppressed, judging the poor;

Lord of wisdom, lord of mercy; most loving, opener of every eye, source of joy, in whose goodness the gods rejoice, thou whose name is hidden.

Thou art the one, maker of all that is, the one; the only one; maker of gods and men; giving food to all.

Hail to thee, thou one with many heads; sleepless when all others sleep, adoration to thee.

HYMN TO AMUN-RA
(*Continued*)

Hail to thee from all creatures from every land, from the height of heaven, from the depth of the sea.
The spirits thou hast made extol thee, saying, welcome to thee, father of the fathers of the gods; we worship thy spirit which is in us.

PRAYER OF THE SOWER

(Finnish)

BLESSING to the seed I scatter,
Where it falls upon the meadow,
By the grace of Ukko mighty,
Through the open finger spaces
Of the hand that all things fashioned.
Queen of meadow-land and pasture!
Bid the earth unlock her treasures.
Bid the soil the young seed nourish,
Never shall their teeming forces
Never shall their strength prolific
Fail to nourish and sustain us
If the Daughters of Creation,
They, the free and bounteous givers
Still extend their gracious favor
Offer still their strong protection.
Rise, O Earth! from out thy slumbers
Bid the soil unlock her treasures!

HYMN TO PANU
(*Finnish*)

(Panu, God of fire, child of the Sun-mother)

O PANU,
Son of the Sun!
Offspring thou of the dear day.
Lift the fire up to the sky.
In the middle of the golden ring,
Within the rock of copper,
Carry it as a child to its mother
Into the lap of the ancient mother.
Place the fire to shine by day,
And to rest at night.
Let it rise every morning!
Let it rest every evening!

THE SALUTATION OF THE DAWN

(*Hindu*)

LISTEN to the exhortation of the Dawn!
Look to this Day! For it is Life,
  The very Life of Life.
In its brief course lie all the Varieties
And Realities of your Existence;
  The Bliss of Growth,
  The Glory of Action,
  The Splendor of Beauty;
For Yesterday is but a Dream,
And To-morrow is only a Vision;
  But To-day well lived
Makes every Yesterday a Dream of Happiness,
And every To-morrow a Vision of Hope.
Look well therefore to this Day!
Such is the Salutation of the Dawn.

PRAYER TO BUDDHA

(Hindu)

THOU in whom innumerable creatures believe!

Thou, Buddha, Victor over the hosts of evil!

Thou, all-wise Being, come down to our world!

Made perfect and glorified by innumerable by-gone revolutions; always pitiful, always gracious toward all creatures!

Look down upon us; for the time has come to pour out blessings on all creatures.

Be gracious to us from thy throne built in thy heavenly world.

Thou art the eternal redemption of all creatures, therefore bow down to us with all thy unstained heavenly societies.

HYMN TO AGNI

(*Hindu*)

(Agni, god of fire in every form, worshipped in every manifestation—sun, lightning, earth, fire—also adored as the spark of life in all of growth, is here invoked as both the sacred flame on the altar, and the highest priest officiating)

I IMPLORE Agni, the chief priest, the divine minister of the sacrifice, the Hotri priest, the best giver of wealth.

Agni, worthy to be implored by former poets and by new, may he bring the gods hither!

Through Agni man gained wealth, satisfying even day by day, glorious wealth of vigorous kindred.

Agni, the offering which thou encirclest on all sides, that alone goes to the gods.

Agni, the Hotri priest, the wise counsellor, the truthful, the most glorious, may he, the God, come with the gods!

Whatever wealth thou, Agni, shalt bestow on the sacrificer, thine it will be, forsooth, Agni.

HYMN TO AGNI
(Continued)

To thee, O Agni, we come day by day, bringing praise in mind, O Illuminator of Darkness!

To thee, the Lord of sacrifices, the bright Guarder of the Law, who art growing in thy own house.

Thou then, O Agni, be gracious to us like as a father to his son; stay with us for our welfare!

PRAYER OF THE GAMBLER

(*Hindu*)

THESE dice that have grown in the air on the great Vibhidaka tree, drive me wild when they roll on the board! This Vibhidaka seems to me intoxicating like a draught of Soma that has grown on Mount Mugovat.

When I think that I shall not play with them again, then am I left by my friends who go afar. But when the brown dice are thrown down and utter speech, then I rush to their rendezvous, like a love-sick maid.

These dice hook, prick, undo, burn and inflame. After the gift of childish playthings they ruin the winner; yet to the gambler they are covered with honey.

They do not bend before the anger of the mighty, even the king bends down before them.

PRAYER OF THE GAMBLER

(*Continued*)

Though having no hands, they resist him who has hands. These playing coals, though cold, when thrown on the board, burn the heart through and through!

Make other friends, O dice—have mercy on us! Do not bewitch us with powerful enchantment! May your wrath abate, and your enmity—let some one else be held in the power of the brown dice!

PRAYER TO KAMI-DANA

(Japanese)

REVERENTLY adoring the great god of the two palaces of Ise,........................

....

......and the gods of the branch temples and branch palaces, and Sohodo no kami, whom I have invited to the shrine set upon this divine altar, and to whom I offer praises day by day.

I pray with awe that they will deign to correct the unwitting faults, which, heard and seen by them, I have committed, and blessing and favoring me according to the powers which they severally wield, cause me to follow the divine example and to perform good works in the Way.

(The House God)

PRAYER OF THE SINGER

(Mexican)

IN THE place of tears, I, the singer, watch my flowers, they enthrall my spirit as I walk alone with them—My spirit sad amid the flowers.

In this spot where the herbage is as sweet ointment, and green as the turquoise and emerald, I dream of a song of beauty while the blossoms of beauty are in my hand!

Let us rejoice now, O friends! O children! For the life of the earth-born is not long upon earth.

I now go forth in swiftness—to the sweet songs I go forth—to the flowers of fragrance, O friends! O children!

O hé! I sang aloud, O hé! I rained song blossoms as I sped!

Let us go forth to the four ways! I, the singer, shall find and bring

PRAYER OF THE SINGER
(Continued)

forth the flowers. Let us be glad while we live—hark to my song of joy!

I, the poet, cry out a song for a place of joy—a radiant song which descends to the Underworld, and there turns and echoes back to you!

I seek neither vestments or riches, O friends! O children! but a song for a place of joy!"

HYMN OF TLA-LOC

(*Mexican*)

(Tla-loc is the God of Storms. He dwells in Tlalocan where the spirits of the elements toss the balls of thunder, and cast the reeds of lightning. This is a masked dramatized ceremony to the rain god)

Priests

TO OUR land the god appears! His banner unfolds to the Four Ways and no one weeps!"

Tla-loc

"I, the god, have returned again! I have turned again to the place of abundance of sacrifices. Westward, when the day grows old I am beheld as a god."

High Priest

"Thy work is that of a magician divine! Truly thou hast made thyself to be of our flesh. Thou hast made thyself, and who dare affront thee?"

Tla-loc

"Truly he who affronts me faces the dangers; My fathers took by the heads the tigers and serpents!"

HYMN OF TLA-LOC
(*Continued*)

Priests

"In Tla-locan, the Place of the Divine, they play at ball! They cast the reeds!"

High Priest to Devotees

"Go forth! Go forth to where the clouds are spread—where the thick mist marks the cloudy house of Tla-loc!"

Tla-loc

"Go ye out to seek me! Seek for the voice I send forth as I rise—a terrible god—a cry on the winds!"

HYMN TO THE ALL-MOTHER

(*Mexican*)

(This goddess is Teteo-inan, the "Mother of Gods" —also known by another name meaning "Heart of the Earth." Her chief temple was on the spot selected by the early missionaries for the "Lady of Guadaloupe" to make her appearance, and the native shrine was razed to make way for the temple of the imported cult of Christendom)

HAIL to our Mother who makes the yellow flowers to bloom— who scatters the seeds of the maguey as she comes from the Land Divine!

Hail to our Mother who casts forth white flowers in abundance!

Hail to our Mother who shines in the thorn bush as a bright butterfly!

Ho! She is our Mother—the woman god of the earth. In the desert she feeds the wild beasts, and gives them to live.

Thus—thus you see her ever abundant in gifts to all flesh.

And as you see the goddess of earth give to the beasts, so also she is giving to the green herbs and the fishes.

Hail to our Mother who casts forth yellow flowers to the sun from the Land Divine!

HYMN OF THE GOD OF FLOWERS

(*Mexican*)

(High Priest, masked as the god, chants)
(Kin-teotl—God of maize)
(Tla-loc—God of storms and the wide plains)

O FRIENDS! The quetzal bird sings—it sings its song at midnight to Kin-teotl.

The god now hears my song by night, he will hear my song as the night brings in the dawn.

I send forth the priests to the house of Tla-loc.

The priests to the house of Tla-loc do I send forth.

I shall go forth to the plains. I shall join myself to them. I shall go where is Kin-teotl. I shall follow the trail to him.

The priests go forth to the house of Tla-loc, to the home of the god of the plains!

PRAYER TO THE MEXICAN GOD OF FIRE

(*Mexican*)

(A victim is sacrificed for rain in the temple of the Earth Fire—a crater of a volcano)

Victim

"IN THE Hall of Flame let me not put to shame my ancestors; decending there let me not put you to shame!

"I fasten a rope to the sacred tree. I twist it in eight folds, that by it, I, a magician, may descend to the magical house."

Priests

"Begin your song in the Hall of Flames! Begin your song in the Hall of Flames!"

Devotees

"Why does not the magician come forth?
Why does he not rise up?"

Priests

"Let his subjects assist in the Hall of Flames!
He appears! He appears! Let his subjects assist!"

PRAYER TO THE MEXICAN GOD OF FIRE
(*Continued*)

"Let his servants never cease the song of the Hall of Flames—let them rejoice greatly—let them dance wonderfully!

(To the victim)

Call ye for the Woman with Abundant Hair, whose care is the Mist and the Rain; call ye for Her!"

THE PRAYER OF THE MAIZE

(*Mexican*)

(This is a conventional ceremony where a high priest, masked, personates Kin-teotl, god of the maize. An altar priest chants of the loves and greatness of the gods, but with an earthly love in his heart for a vestal who personates the goddess of art in a similar ceremony at the adjacent temple of Cholula)

Priest

(Placing flowers of the field on shrine)

THE FLOWER in my heart blossoms, sweetness it brings in the night!

Our mother has loved. The goddess of love has scattered flowers of fragrance!"

Kin-teotl

"I, Kin-teotl, god of the grain, am as a flower—a flower ever renewing!"

Priest

"Kin-teotl was born from the water, he came as a mortal, as a youth, from the cerulean home of the fishes, an ever new, glorious god!

He shone as the sun; his mother dwelt in the House of the Dawn!"

THE PRAYER OF THE MAIZE

(Continued)

Kin-teotl

"I come forth on the earth—even to the market place like a mortal —even I—great and glorious!

Be ye happy under the flower bush varied in hue as the quetzal bird; Listen to the quechol singing to the gods! Listen to the singing of the quechol along the river:— hear its flute along the river in the home of the reeds!"

(The flutes sound the call of the birds as Kin-teotl disappears in the temple followed by the devotees)

Priest

"Ai!—would that my altar flowers would cease from dying! Our flesh is as flowers—even as flowers in the place of the flowers.

She goes to the mart! As goddess they carry her to the mart! She speaks at Cholula—she startles my heart! She startles my heart!

THE PRAYER OF THE MAIZE

(*Continued*)

"Ai! for joy the high priest is there
at her shrine! Where merchants
sell the ear rings of green jade, she
is to be seen by men—in the
Place of Wonders she is to be
seen!
Sleep, sleep, sleep! I fold my hands
to sleep!
I, O Woman!—sleep!"

HYMN TO CIHUA-COATL
(*Mexican*)

(Cihua-coatl, mythic, mother of earth-born people)

SERPENT Woman, plumed with eagle feathers, with the crest of eagles, comes, beating her drum, from the Place of the Old.

She alone, who is our flesh, goddess of the fields and shrubs, is strong to support us.

Our mother is as twelve eagles, goddess of drums calling the gods, filling the fields.

She is our mother—a goddess of war, our mother, a companion from the Home of Ancestors.

She comes forth, she appears when war is waged, she protects us in war that we be not destroyed—an example and companion from the Home of the Ancestors.

She comes adorned in the ancient manner with the eagle's crest,—in the ancient manner with the eagle's crest!

PRAYER TO THE GOD OF THIEVES

(South Pacific Island)

O THOU divine Outre-reter!
We go out for plunder.
Cause all things to sleep in the house.
Owner of the house, sleep on!
Threshold of the house, sleep on!
Little insects of the house, sleep on!
Central - post, ridge - pole, rafters, thatch of the house, sleep on!
O Rongo, grant us success!

INVOCATION TO ORMAZD

(*Persian*)

IN THE name of God, the giver, forgiver, rich in love, praise be to the name of Ormazd, the God with the name who always was, always is, and always will be; the heavenly among the heavenly, with the name—"From whom alone is derived rule."

With all strength bring I thanks.

All good do I accept at thy command O God, and think, and speak, and do it. I believe in the pure law; by every good work seek I forgiveness for all sins. I keep pure the six powers—thought, speech, work, memory, mind and understanding. According to thy will am I able to accomplish. O accomplisher of good, thy honor, with good thoughts, good works.

I enter on the shining way to Paradise; may the fearful terror of

INVOCATION TO ORMAZD

(Continued)

hell not overcome me! May I step over the bridge Chinevat. May I attain Paradise with much perfume, and all brightness.

Praise be to the Overseer, the Lord, who rewards those who accomplish good deeds according to his own wish, and at last purifies even the wicked ones of hell.

MOHAMMEDAN PRAYER OF ADORATION

(*Persian*)

SOUL of the Soul! Neither thought nor reason comprehend thy essence, and no one knows thy attributes.

Souls have no idea of thy being. The prophets themselves sink in the dust of thy road.

Although intellect exists by thee, has it ever yet found the path of thy existence?

O thou, who art in the interior and in the exterior of the soul! Thou art and thou art not that which I say.

In thy presence reason grows dizzy; it loses the thread that would direct it in thy way.

I perceive clearly the universe in thee, and yet discover thee not in the world.

MOHAMMEDAN PRAYER OF ADORATION
(*Continued*)

All beings are marked with thy impress, but thyself hast no impress visible;

Thou reservest the secret of thine existence.

AN INCA'S DEATH PRAYER

(*Peruvian*)

O CREATOR of men
Thy servant speaks.
Then look on him
The king of Cusco.

Do not forget me
O thou noble creator.
O thou of my dreams.
Dost thou forget
And I on the point of death?
Wilt thou ignore my prayer
Or wilt thou make known
Who thou art?
Thou mayest be what I thought,
Yet perchance thou art a phantom,
A thing that causes fear.
Oh, if I might know!
Oh, if it could be revealed!
Thou who made me out of earth,
And of clay formed me.
Oh look upon me!
Who art thou, O Creator?
Now I am very old.

HYMN TO THE UNKNOWN GOD

(*Peruvian*)

O RULER! Lord of the universe,
Whether thou art male,
Whether thou art female,
Lord of reproduction
Wherever thou mayest be!
O Lord of divination
Where art thou?
Thou mayest be above,
Thou mayest be below,
Or perhaps around
Thy splendid throne and sceptre.
O hear me!
From the sky above,
In which thou mayest be,
From the sea beneath
In which thou mayest be.
Creator of the world,
Maker of all men;
Lord of all Lords
My eyes fail me for longing to see
thee
For the sole desire to know thee.

HYMN TO THE UNKNOWN GOD
(Continued)

O look down upon me
For thou knowest me.
The sun—the moon—
The day—the night—
Spring—winter,
Are not ordained in vain
By thee, O Deity!
They all travel
To the assigned place;
They all arrive
At their destined ends
Whithersoever thou pleasest.
Thy royal sceptre
Thou holdest.
O hear me!
O choose me!
Let it not be
That I should tire,
That I should die!

BIBLIOGRAPHY

Apache Prayer, from *The North American Indian*, by special permission of Edward S. Curtis.

A partial list of the other scholars and works to whom the compiler is indebted:

Daniel G. Brinton, *Rig Veda Americana.*

Françoise Lenormant, *La Magie chez les Chaldées.*

F. Max Muller, *Physical Religion.*

Washington Matthews, *Navajo Legends.*

Sir Clements Markham, *Incas of Peru.*

Records of the Past.

Bernardino de Sahagun, *Historia de las cosas de la Nueva Espana.*

A. H. Sayce, *Babylonian Exorcism.*

H. Fox Talbot, *Biblical Archaeology.*

The Egyptian *Book of the Dead.*

The *Kalevala.*

The *Zend Avesta.*